BEASTS AND THE BATTLEFIELD

# BEASTLY ARMOR

## MILITARY DEFENSES INSPIRED BY ANIMALS

Charles C. Hofer

CAPSTONE PRESS
a capstone imprint

Captivate is published by Capstone Press, an imprint of Capstone.
1710 Roe Crest Drive, North Mankato, Minnesota 56003
www.capstonepub.com

Copyright © 2020 by Capstone. All rights reserved. No part of this publication may be reproduced in whole or in part, or stored in a retrieval system, or transmitted in any form or by any means, electronic, mechanical, photocopying, recording, or otherwise, without written permission of the publisher

**Library of Congress Cataloging-in-Publication data is available on the Library of Congress website.**
ISBN: 978-1-5453-9020-3 (hardcover)
ISBN: 978-1-4966-6590-4 (paperback)
ISBN: 978-1-5435-9025-8 (ebook PDF)

Summary: Describes how military armor and defenses have been inspired by animals and nature from ancient times until today.

**Editorial Credits**
Aaron Sautter, editor; Kyle Grenz, designer; Morgan Walters, media researcher; Katy LaVigne, production specialist

**Image Credits**
Flickr: U.S. Army photo by Tom Faulkner, bottom left 20; Getty Images: IWM/Getty Images, 17, U.S. Navy, 19; Newscom: Album / Metropolitan Museum of Art, NY, bottom right 9, De Agostini / G. Dagli Orti Universal Images Group, (statue) 13; Shutterstock: AlejandroCarnicero, 25, alessandro guerriero, (man) 11, Alexander Tolstykh, 23, Anton Kozyrev, (beetle) 28, arka38, 4, Avatar_023, (vest) Cover, Borhax, (map) 5, BPTU, 26, Cristina Romero Palma, bottom right 20, Dan Thornberg, (arrow) 8, Dawid Lech, middle 15, Dzha33, (helmet) 7, Everett Historical, 14, Getmilitaryphotos, (soldier) 7, top 21 , bottom 21 (soldier) 28, (man) 29, GUDKOV ANDREY, (whale) 29, Howard Barnes, 16, Iakov Filimonov, (elk) 8, Joop Hoek, top 22, luca85, (shell) Cover, Mark_Kostich, 10, mountainpix, bottom left 9, MyImages - Micha, top 15, NaturePhoto, 27, Neirfy, (dolphin) 18, Nosyrevy, (fish) 11, Number1411, (beetle) 13, Omelchenko, design element throughout, pets in frames, (turtle) 7, Samakai, top right 24, Shahnewaz Mahmood, bottom left 18, silver tiger, (droplets) 28, Sofiaworld, top left 24, Umlaut1968, (tank) 5, vvoe, bottom 22, Wendy Naepflin, (samurai) 13

All internet sites appearing in back matter were available and accurate when this book was sent to press.

Printed and bound in the United States of America.
PA99

# Table of Contents

**Inspired by Nature** ..................... **4**

**Ancient Defenses** ...................... **8**

**Defenses in the Modern Age** ........................... **14**

**The Future is Now!** ................... **20**

> Glossary ................................ 30
> Read More ............................. 31
> Internet Links ........................ 31
> Index ..................................... 32

Words in **bold** are in the glossary.

# Inspired by Nature

More than 100 years ago in 1915, a new machine rumbled onto the battlefield. It was large and slow. But it went where most vehicles could not. It was made from thick metal. It did not have wheels. Instead, it had **tracks** that gripped the ground. It was the first tank.

In World War I (1914–1918), wheeled vehicles often got stuck in the mud. But a tank's tracks act like a caterpillar's legs. The tracks help tanks move through mud and over objects.

Tanks have come a long way since World War I. But the main design has stayed the same. And it's all thanks to the tiny caterpillar.

## FACT

The Allied Powers defeated the Central Powers to win World War I. The Central Powers included the countries of Germany, Austria-Hungary, and Turkey. The Allied Powers included France, Great Britain, Italy, the United States, and other countries.

- Allied Powers
- Central Powers
- Neutral countries

tank tracks

## Copying Nature

In the wild, animals must compete to survive. Some animals have sharp claws or teeth. Others have strong defenses to protect themselves. Some animals, like tortoises, might have a hard shell. Some can fly. Others are good at hiding.

Military scientists study animals closely to invent new weapons and gear. It makes sense. Animals have developed their natural skills over millions of years. Scientists use what they learn to make new defenses for soldiers. Copying nature this way is called **biomimicry**. Animals have sparked many ideas for better armor, **camouflage**, robots, and more.

However, copying from nature is nothing new. Armies have done it for thousands of years. Throughout history, nature has provided new ideas to protect soldiers in the armed forces.

> **FACT**
> The word "biomimicry" comes from two ancient Greek words. *Bios* means "life," and *mimesis* means "to imitate" or copy.

Helmets are hard like a tortoise shell.

camouflage uniform

# Ancient Defenses

## The First Armor

Long ago, people used bows and arrows or clubs. Some used stone axes. These weapons were simple. But they were still deadly. People needed protection.

arrow with stone tip

Animals provided skins to make leather armor and shields.

Humans made the first defenses directly from animals. They **tanned** animal skins. This process turns animal skins into leather. They used hardened leather to make simple body armor and shields. It helped protect fighters from simple weapons.

Leather armor and shields worked well for a long time. But leather wouldn't last. It was later replaced by a stronger material—metal.

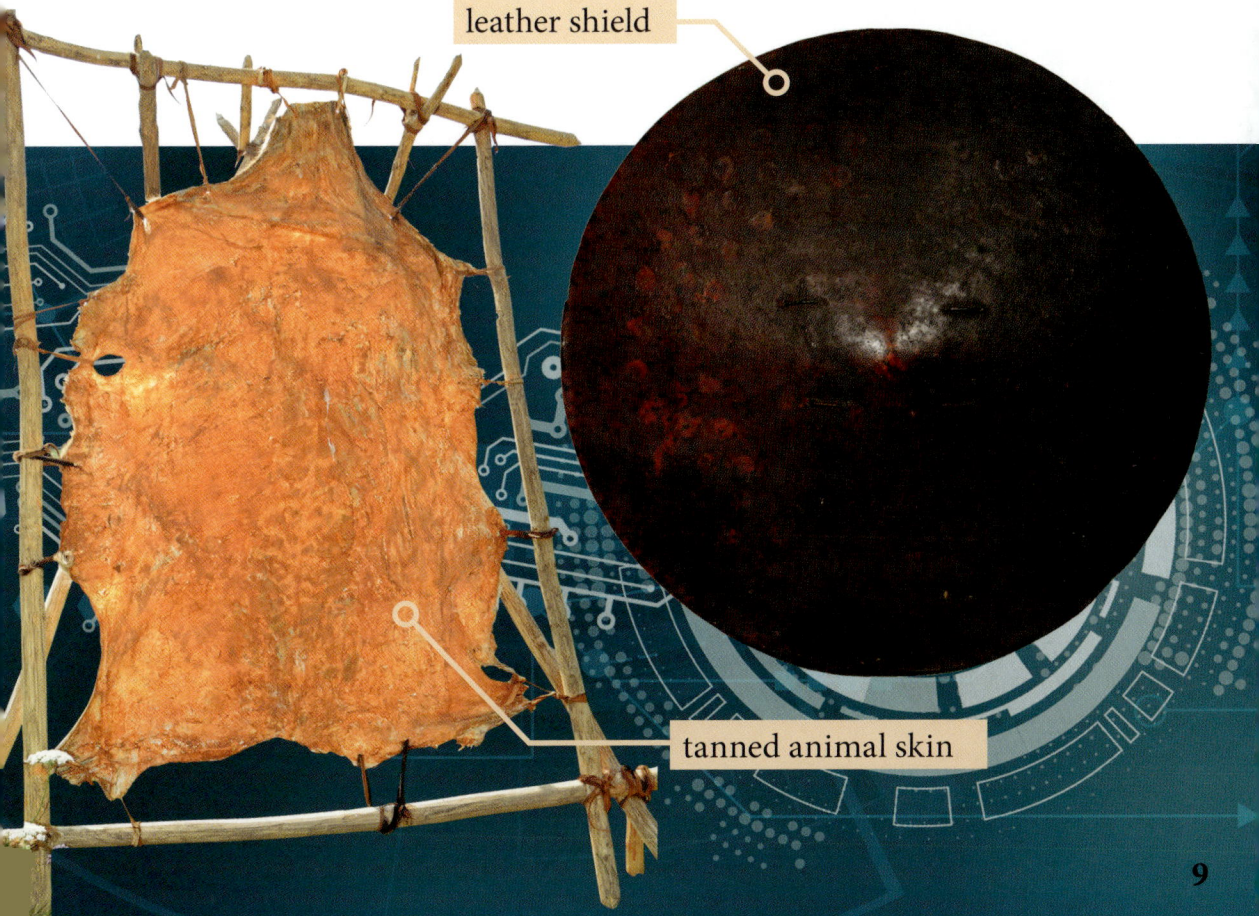

leather shield

tanned animal skin

## The Age of Metal

Thousands of years ago, people began making metal tools from bronze and iron. They also made strong metal axes, swords, and spears. Defenses had to become stronger.

The first metal armor was called scale armor. It imitated reptile scales. It was made with small, overlapping metal plates. It worked well against blows from heavy weapons.

Soldiers later wore chain mail armor. It was made of small iron rings linked together. This armor acted like fish scales. It was lightweight and flexible. Soldiers could move and fight easily in chain mail.

Knights in Europe wore full suits of armor. The metal suits acted like an insect's **exoskeleton**. This hard outer layer of an insect's body protects it from enemies. Armored suits protected knights during battle.

Scale armor acted like a snake's scales.

## FACT

Roman soldiers used the tortoise formation. They gathered together and overlapped their metal shields. This move formed a shell-like structure to protect the soldiers.

Chain mail was like fish scales.

Solid armor acted like an insect's hard outer shell.

## Fear as Defense

Metal armor was useful in battle. But sometimes making enemies fear you could work just as well. Armed forces copied nature to do this too.

The samurai were Japanese warriors. Some wore helmets with large horns like a deer. Other helmets looked like scary horned beetles. Enemy soldiers often ran from these frightening helmets.

In Central America the Aztec people respected strong animals. Jaguar Knights and Eagle Warriors were fierce fighters. They wore armor covered with feathers, furs, and claws. They also wore frightening helmets that looked like these mighty beasts.

### The End of Heavy Armor

Gunpowder was invented more than 1,000 years ago. Armies soon learned to use it in cannons, bombs, and guns. Heavy armor suits didn't work well against these powerful weapons. About 200 years ago, troops stopped wearing much armor. They wanted to move faster in battle. Soldiers mainly wore just metal helmets to protect their heads.

Some samurai helmets had horns like a rhinoceros beetle.

Aztec Eagle Warrior

# Advancing Defenses

## Looking to the Sky

By 1900 battlefields became even more deadly. To protect troops, military defenses had to change once again. The newest defenses would soon be found in the sky.

Humans had long dreamed about flying. Then Orville and Wilbur Wright invented the first successful airplane in 1903. They shaped the plane's wings like a bird's wings. The shape allowed the plane to lift off the ground. Airplanes would soon change battlefields forever.

Wright brothers' *Flyer II* in 1904

A biplane's wings imitate the shape of bird wings.

Flying above enemies gives armies a big advantage in battle. Early in World War I, airplanes were used only for defense. Pilots flew high to find enemies. They sent information back to their ground troops. Leaders could then form a useful battle plan.

## Hiding in Plain Sight

The ocean was another dangerous battlefield in World War I. German U-boats destroyed many British ships. These **submarines** often attacked without warning.

The British Navy found an amazing solution. They studied how zebra stripes confuse **predators**, such as lions. This gives zebras extra time to escape.

Striped ships looked like a group of zebras.

The navy followed nature's example. It began painting ships in black and white stripes. They called it dazzle camouflage. Almost 3,000 British ships were painted this way. The plan worked. The number of U-boat attacks soon dropped. The bold patterns confused U-boat crews. This gave British ships time to get away.

## Beneath the Waves

Some animals have natural **sonar** called **echolocation**. Dolphins make squeak and click sounds. The sounds bounce off fish back to the dolphins. Hearing the sounds helps them locate food in the ocean.

Sonar works in the same way. Sound waves are sent out that bounce off objects. The speed of the returning waves is then measured. This information helps find hidden rocks, bombs, or other objects in the water.

Sonar works like a dolphin's echolocation.

**FACT**
The U.S. Navy began training dolphins about 50 years ago. They carry cameras and use their sonar to find underwater bombs.

Ships first used sonar more than 100 years ago. It helped find hidden icebergs. Armed forces soon learned to use it too. During World War I, sonar helped find submarines.

# The Future Is Now!

Today's soldiers fight in every corner of the world. And they don't just fight the enemy. They often must survive extreme heat, cold, and dry conditions. Thanks to animals, their defenses are becoming better than ever. Many new inventions are helping protect troops on the battlefield.

## Future Machines

Many future defenses are being made by the Defense Advanced Research Projects Agency, or DARPA. Scientists at DARPA work on amazing new inventions based on nature. One example is the Soft Exosuit. It works like an insect's exoskeleton. It gives soldiers extra support to carry heavy loads over long distances.

An exosuit provides extra support like a beetle's exoskeleton.

soldier in cold-weather gear

soldier in warm-weather gear

## Stronger, Faster, Lighter

Soldiers may soon have tough new armor. And it's thanks to some of nature's most unusual animals. Mollusks are simple creatures. But they have tough shells. Their shells protect them from pounding ocean waves and hungry predators.

mollusks

Scientists have long known about mollusk shells. But they have been difficult to copy. Now, thanks to **3-D printers**, scientists can copy the mollusk's special shell design. They hope to soon design new armor and helmets that are lighter and stronger.

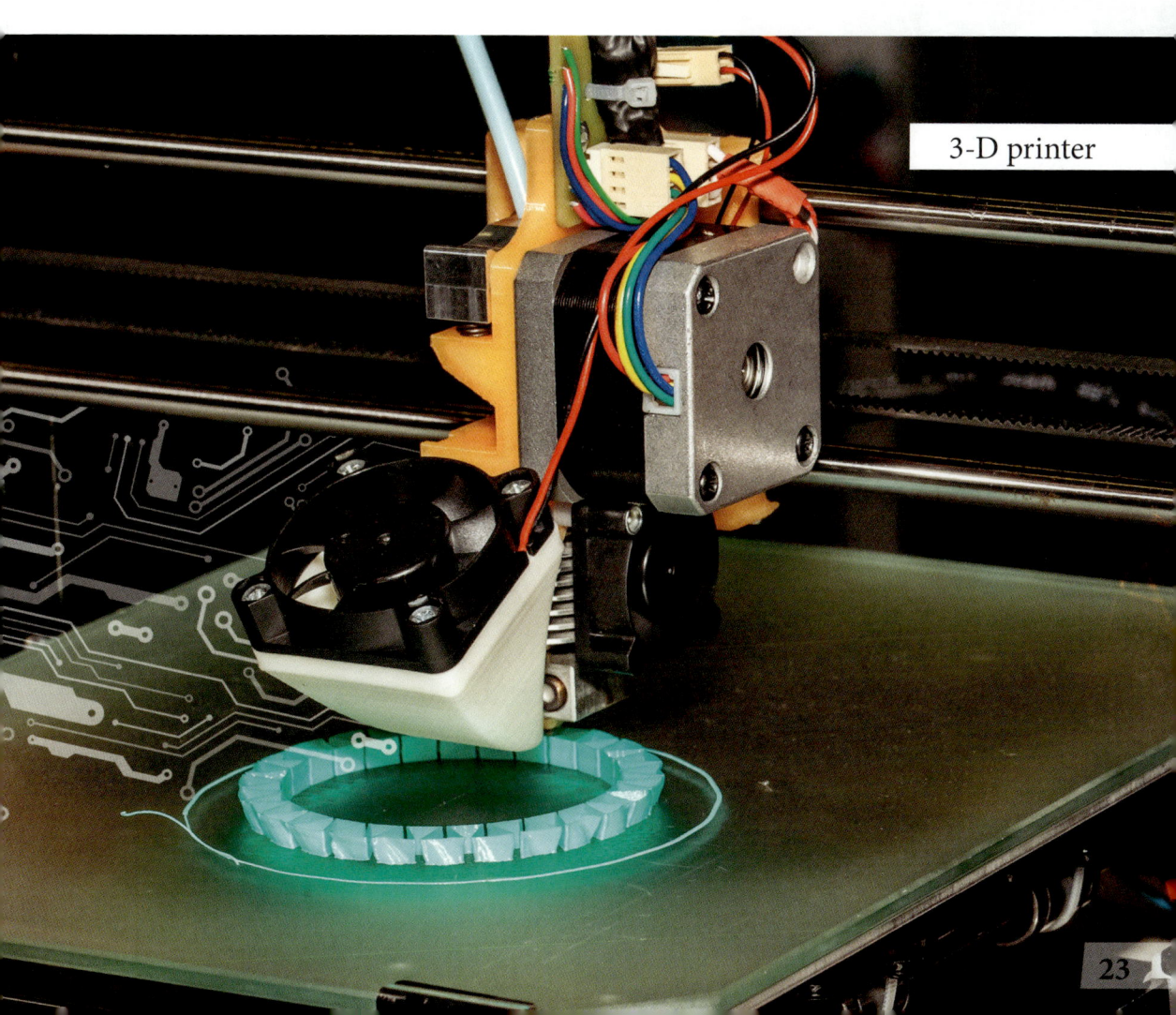

3-D printer

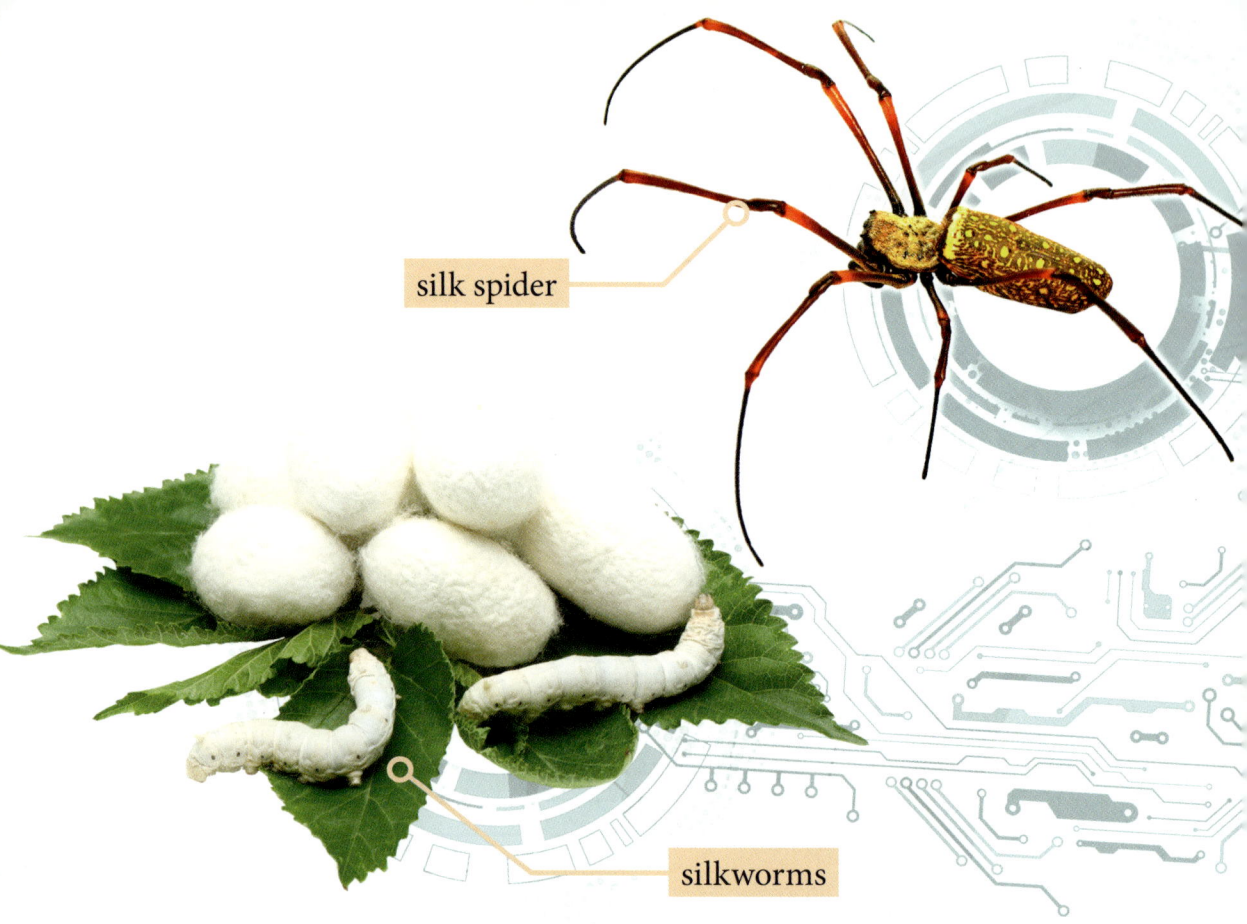

silk spider

silkworms

## The Strength of Silk

Silk is made by spiders and silkworms. It is used to make cloth that is lightweight but strong. After World War I, pilots began using silk **parachutes**. If their planes were shot down, pilots needed a safe way to return to the ground.

Silk is playing a role in new defenses too. The U.S. Air Force is testing silk made from new materials. It is lightweight and even stronger than natural silk. Researchers hope to use the new silk to make armor that is lightweight and cool.

## Next-Level Camo

Like many animals, soldiers often use camouflage to hide from enemies. Today scientists are working to design the camo of tomorrow. They're studying Earth's strangest creatures to do it.

> **FACT**
> Researchers are also working to hide a person's body heat. New uniforms may help troops hide when enemies use heat-sensing equipment.

soldier in camouflage

Some ocean animals, such as squids and octopuses, can change color in seconds. Sometimes they even make their skin appear rough or smooth. This helps them blend in with the area around them.

The U.S. military is working to copy this ability. Future uniforms may change color instantly. They will help soldiers hide on the battlefield.

octopus

## Survive!

In Africa's Namib Desert, darkling beetles have special shells. They are covered in tiny bumps. The shell can collect moisture from the air. The water then drips into the beetle's mouth. Scientists are working to copy the beetle's shell. If successful, new water-collecting gear could help soldiers survive in dry deserts.

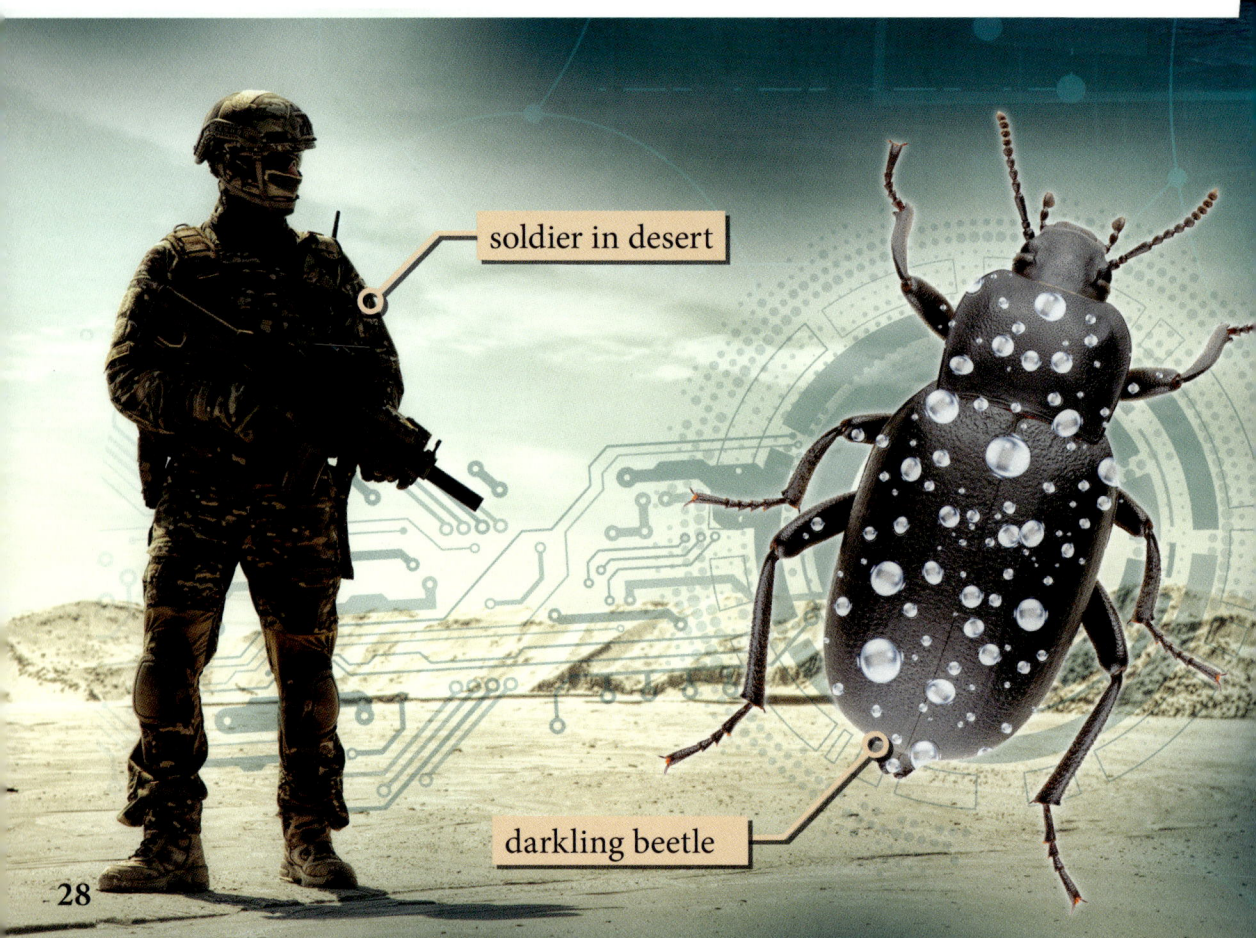

Future wetsuits may help hold body heat like a whale's blubber.

Scientists are designing new wetsuits based on nature. Penguin feathers trap body heat. Whales and dolphins have a thick layer of blubber, or fat, that traps heat. Future wetsuits may copy these animals. New materials can better trap body heat. The new wetsuits will help troops survive in freezing waters.

Scientists are working hard to invent tomorrow's defenses. Armed forces have relied on Mother Nature's defenses for a long time. Who knows what nature-based gear will be invented next?

# Glossary

**3-D printer** (THREE-dee PRIN-tur)—a device that uses a computer program to create objects

**biomimicry** (by-oh-MIH-mih-kree)—copying the design of a living thing

**camouflage** (KA-muh-flahzh)—patterns or colors that help animals or people to blend in with the area around them

**echolocation** (eh-koh-loh-KAY-shuhn)—the process of using sounds and echoes to locate objects

**exoskeleton** (ek-soh-SKE-luh-tuhn)—the hard outer shell of an insect

**parachute** (PAIR-uh-shoot)—a large piece of cloth used to float slowly and safely to the ground

**predator** (PRED-uh-tur)—an animal that hunts other animals for food

**sonar** (SOH-nar)—a device that uses sound waves to find underwater objects; sonar stands for sound navigation and ranging

**submarine** (SUHB-muh-reen)—a ship that can travel under the water

**tan** (TAN)—to clean, treat, and dry animal skins to turn them into leather

**track** (TRAK)—the links that form a loop on which some vehicles travel

# Read More

Johnson, Rebecca L. *When Lunch Fights Back: Wickedly Clever Animal Defenses.* Minneapolis: Millbrook Press, 2015.

Koontz, Robin Michal. *Nature-Inspired Contraptions.* North Mankato, MN: Rourke Educational Media, 2019.

Miller, Tessa. *Creepy & Crawly: Technology Inspired by Animals.* Minneapolis: Lerner Publishing, 2018.

# Internet Links

*Beetle-Inspired Water Bottle*
https://stemazing.org/beetle-inspired-water-bottle/

*The Biomimicry Institute*
https://biomimicry.org

*Defense Advanced Research Projects Agency*
https://www.darpa.mil

# Index

3-D printers, 23

animal defenses, 6
animals
    bats, 18
    birds, 14
    caterpillars, 4
    darkling beetles, 28
    deer, 12
    dolphins, 18, 19, 29
    fish, 10
    horned beetles, 12
    mollusks, 22–23
    octopuses, 27
    penguins, 29
    reptiles, 10
    silkworms, 24
    spiders, 24
    squids, 27
    tortoises, 6, 11
    whales, 29
    zebras, 16
animal skins, 9
armor, 9, 10, 12
Aztec Warriors, 12

biomimicry, 6

camouflage, 6, 26
    dazzle camouflage, 17

Defense Advanced Research Projects Agency (DARPA), 20

echolocation, 18
exoskeletons, 10, 20

gunpowder, 12

helmets, 12

military defenses, 6, 9, 10, 11, 14, 15, 20, 24, 29

Namib Desert, 28

scientists, 6, 20, 23, 26, 28, 29
shields, 9, 11
special gear
    parachutes, 24
    silk, 24
    Soft Exosuit, 20
    sonar, 18–19
    uniforms, 26, 27
    water collectors, 28
    wetsuits, 29

vehicles
    airplanes, 14, 15
    submarines, 16–17, 19
    tanks, 4

World War I, 4, 5, 15, 16, 19, 24
Wright, Orville and Wilbur, 14